The Coast Book

Dr Brian Knapp

Durdle Dor, Dorset, is an arch cut in limestone rock.

Atlantic Europe Publishing

First published in 2002 by
Atlantic Europe Publishing Company Ltd

Author
Brian Knapp, BSc, PhD
Art Director
Duncan McCrae, BSc
Editors
*Lisa Magloff, BA, Barbara Bass, BA
and Gillian Gatehouse*
Designed and produced by
EARTHSCAPE EDITIONS
Reproduced in Malaysia by
Global Colour
Printed in Hong Kong by
Wing King Tong Company Ltd

The Coast Book – *Curriculum Visions*
A CIP record for this book is
available from the British Library

Hardback ISBN 1 86214 074 X
Paperback ISBN 1 86214 089 8

Illustrations
All illustrations by *David Woodroffe*
except the following: *Nicolas Debon* p5

Picture credits
All photographs are from the Earthscape
Editions photolibrary except the following:
(c=centre t=top b=bottom l=left r=right)
*Image provided by ORBIMAGE © Orbital Imaging
Corporation and processing by NASA Goddard
Space Flight Center* 31bl; *NOAA* 43bl

*This product is manufactured from sustainable
managed forests. For every tree cut down at least
one more is planted.*

Sand and shells from a beach

Curriculum Visions

Curriculum Visions is a registered trademark of
Atlantic Europe Publishing Company Ltd.

Glossary
There is a glossary on pages 46–47.
Glossary terms are referred to in the
text by using CAPITALS.

Index
There is an index on page 48.

Teacher's Guide
There is a Teacher's Guide to
accompany this book, available
only from the publisher.

Posters
Two posters showing the key features of
coastal environments are available as
part of a package only from the publisher.

Dedicated Web Site
There's more about other great Curriculum Visions
packs and a wealth of supporting information
available at our dedicated web site. Visit:

www.CurriculumVisions.com

 ## Take care by coasts!

It is easy to visit coasts to see for yourself many
of the landshapes described in this book. But
remember waves, tides and cliffs can be
dangerous so <u>never</u> take risks near deep water,
or go near the coast in stormy weather.

Contents

Surfing, Wollongong, Australia

Introduction

The coast is where the land meets the sea. It is one of the most rapidly changing parts of the world and contains dramatic scenery. But it is also a place we can easily damage.

❶ Some parts of the **COAST** jut out to make **HEADLANDS**, while in other parts there are sweeping **BAYS**. See how headlands and bays are connected to hard and soft rocks on pages 6 to 11.

❷ **BEACHES** form out of the material worn from cliffs. How this happens and what beach material looks like is shown on pages 12 to 15.

❸ Find out the way **CLIFF** shapes are affected by rocks on pages 16 and 17.

❹ Where rocks are hard, waves find tiny weaknesses and create **CAVES**, **ARCHES** and **STACKS**. Find out how this happens on pages 18 and 19.

❺ **SEA LEVEL** has not always been the same. During an **ICE AGE** it falls dramatically. When it rises, it drowns valleys, as shown on pages 20 and 21.

❻ When **WAVES** break on the beach they rush forward and flow backward. Look at the pattern of waves on pages 22 to 25.

❼ Beaches have many uses. Find out how people use a beach, and when they can damage it, on pages 26 and 27.

❽ When waves break they lift sand off the beach and some of it moves along the beach. Find out how to see the signs of moving sand on pages 28 and 29.

❾ **DELTAS** form where rivers enter the sea. Find out about delta shapes on pages 30 and 31.

❿ If you live close to a crumbling cliff or a stormy beach you may be putting your life at risk. Find out why on pages 32 to 35.

⓫ There are some ways you can protect your home from the sea. Some of them are described on pages 36 and 37.

⓬ What is the future for our coasts? This depends on how we take different points of view into account. Read some views about how to use the coast on pages 38 and 39.

⓭ Many people now think that the best way of protecting the coast is to leave it alone. See why this is on pages 40 and 41.

⓮ Sometimes disasters such as **OIL SPILLS** can **POLLUTE** a beach, making it unpleasant for holidaymakers and a disaster for wildlife. Find out what happens on pages 42 and 43.

⓯ The coast is home to wildlife, too. Find out how they use it on pages 44 and 45.

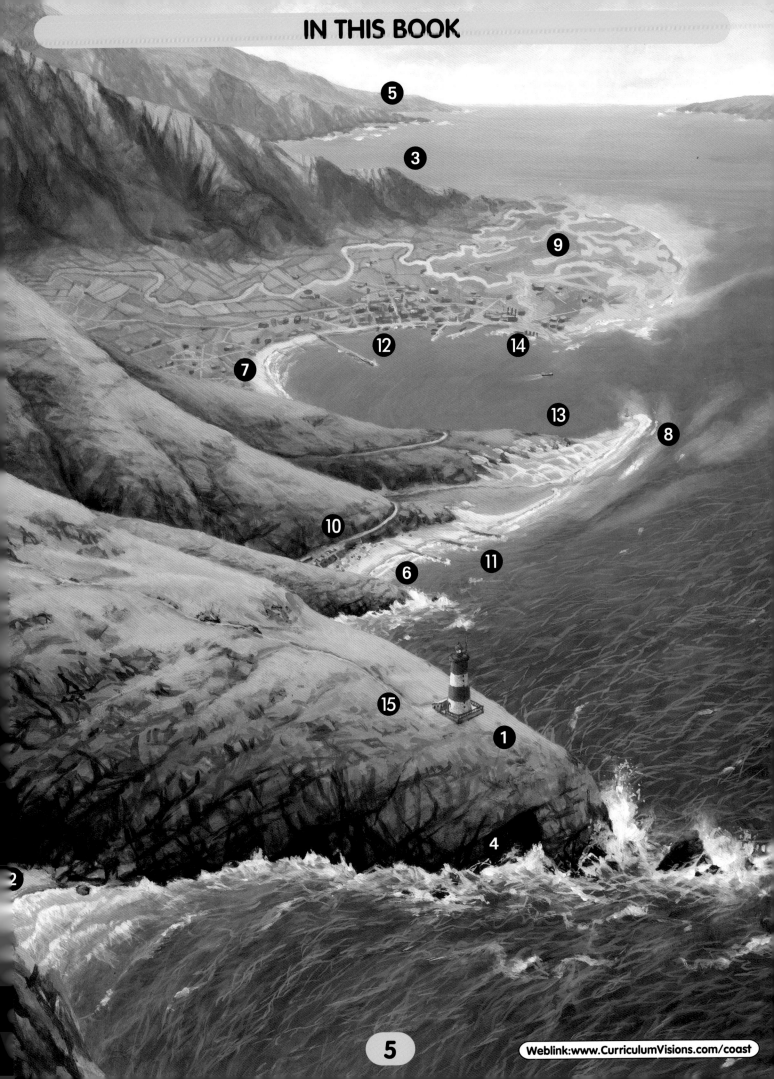

What makes a coast?

A coast, or seaside, is where waves and tides change the shape of the land.

People often use the word seaside when they are talking about the **COAST** (picture ①). It's a good word because it describes exactly where the coast is – the land beside the sea.

Beach

To many people, a seaside holiday means a holiday on the **BEACH** (pictures ② and ③). Many beaches are almost flat and made of sand, or steeper and made of pebbles (shingle). Many beaches are found in **BAYS**.

◄ ② Holidaymakers in Hawaii.

▼ ③ The great expanse of Blackpool sands, Lancashire.

▼ ① This diagram shows that the coast is only the part of the land affected by waves and tides.

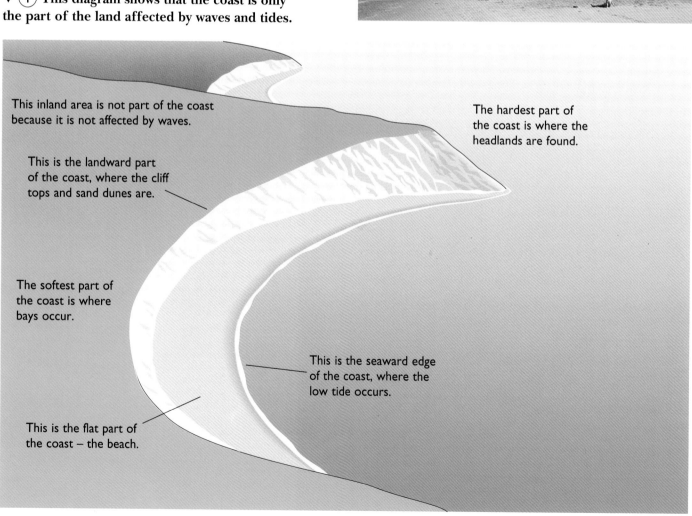

This inland area is not part of the coast because it is not affected by waves.

This is the landward part of the coast, where the cliff tops and sand dunes are.

The hardest part of the coast is where the headlands are found.

The softest part of the coast is where bays occur.

This is the seaward edge of the coast, where the low tide occurs.

This is the flat part of the coast – the beach.

The beach is covered and uncovered each day by the sea. The sea comes and goes because of the effect of the **TIDES**.

Cliff

Another part of the seaside – and a part that fewer people visit – is rocky and has steep slopes. This steep part of the seaside is called a **CLIFF** (picture ④). Most cliffs are found on **HEADLANDS**, although some are also found at the back of bays.

Delta

Some parts of the coast contain **DELTAS**. Deltas are fan-shaped areas of sand found where rivers enter the sea and drop the material they have carried from further inland.

▲ ④ These cliffs are in Cornwall. They are part of a headland.

Estuary

Some parts of the coast are deeply indented (picture ⑤). They are called **ESTUARIES**. Estuaries are important parts of the coast because they provide sheltered harbours.

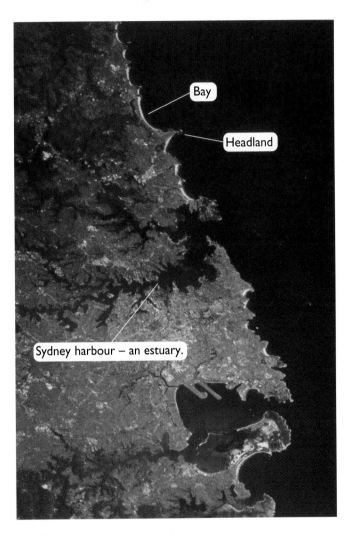

Bay

Headland

Sydney harbour – an estuary.

▲ ⑤ This is the coastline of eastern Australia, near Sydney, as seen from the Space Shuttle.

From high above, the coast is laid out like a map and you can see how different parts of the coast fit together.

In some places the land juts out to form headlands. In between the headlands you can see wide, curved bays. The yellow line along the shoreward side of the bays shows where beaches occur. The large inlets with crinkly edges are estuaries.

Headlands

Where there are hard and soft rocks along a coast, the harder rocks are left standing out as headlands.

Many parts of the coast have areas of hard rocks, separated by areas that are made of softer rocks. Waves can wear away soft rock faster and, as a result, form a coast of headlands and bays.

Headlands

A headland is a part of the coastline that juts out to sea. It is always made of the hardest rock along the coast. This is why it has been able to stand up to the battering of the waves more successfully than the rocks nearby (picture ①).

Because headlands run out to sea, waves can attack them on two sides (pictures ② and ③). This gives the waves a chance to wear away weaker parts of the headland (see also page 14).

The remains of where the headland used to be are often found standing out to sea beyond the present cliffs. They show you how even the hardest rocks at the coast are worn away under the pounding of waves.

Headlands are places of deep water. They get a tremendous battering by waves during storms, and rocks that fall from the cliffs are quickly swept away into the more sheltered parts of the bays. This is why headlands rarely have beaches at their feet. Despite all the pounding, because the rocks in headlands are harder than other parts of the coast, headlands are never worn away completely, but always stand out from bays.

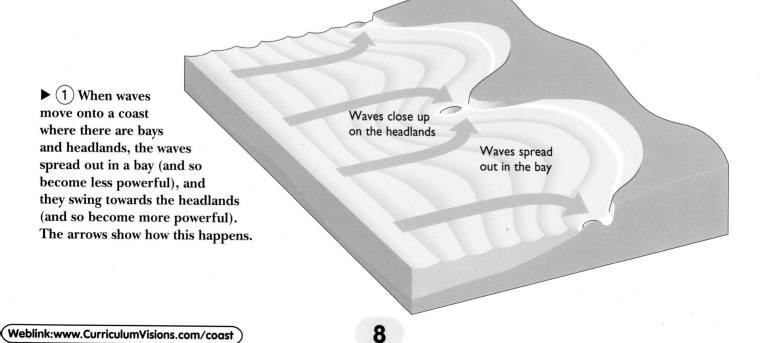

▶ ① **When waves move onto a coast where there are bays and headlands, the waves spread out in a bay (and so become less powerful), and they swing towards the headlands (and so become more powerful). The arrows show how this happens.**

Waves close up on the headlands

Waves spread out in the bay

▲ ② Look into the distance of this picture of the Cornish coast and notice how hard rocks make a headland. In the foreground, the sea is attacking the cliff by wearing away the weaker parts.

▼ ③ In this picture, of the Gower near Swansea, a headland is made of sloping layers of hard rock. This picture was taken at low tide. You can see the high tide line as a 'stain' on the rocks in the foreground. Notice there is no beach.

9

Bays

When there are hard and soft rocks along a coast, the soft rocks get worn away to make bays, while the hard rocks are left standing out as headlands.

Bays are hollowed-out parts of the coast (picture ①), formed where softer rocks are found. Very small bays are called **COVES**.

The size of a bay depends on how much of the coast contains soft rocks.

Bays are more sheltered from storm waves than headlands. At the back of a bay, it is common to find a wide, gently-sloping **BEACH** (picture ②). There may also be **SAND DUNES** (see page 27).

Wide bays

Wide bays, such as those shown in picture ② and picture ① **A**, are the most common type of bay around the coast. They are found where bands of soft rock are exposed to the sea.

▼ ① There are two types of bay: those which are open to the sea (**A**), and those which are almost circular (**B**).

▲ ② This is a bay on the Gower near Swansea, seen at low tide. The wide sandy beach is very clear. The headland in the distance stands out in deep water and has no beach.

Circular bays

Circular bays (pictures ③ and ① **B**) are very picturesque. They occur where a band of hard rock runs beside the coast. The soft rock inland is then only scooped out where waves have broken through the hard rock (picture ④). These bays are not very common.

▼ ④ Here you can see how a band of rock can protect a bay. In the foreground the rock has only partly been worn away and behind it is a circular bay. In the background, the hard rock has been worn entirely away and so the bay is more open. This picture was taken near Durdle Dor.

▼ ③ A few bays are almost circular. This is Lulworth Cove in Dorset.

Circular bay

Soft rocks

Hard rocks

Pounding waves, crashing cliffs

When storm waves pound against the bottom of a cliff, even hard rocks can come crashing down.

Most of us visit the seaside when the weather is fine and the waves splash gently against the rocks. But it is not always like this. If we were to visit the seaside during a storm, we would find huge **WAVES** pounding against the cliffs. This is when rapid change occurs.

The wearing away of a cliff is called **EROSION**. There are two ways that cliffs are worn away. One way is described here; the other way is shown on pages 14 and 15.

Water force

To understand how pounding waves can break up cliffs, just imagine a wave as a moving wall of water.

Water is very heavy. Moving water therefore carries a lot of force with it. As a result, a wave crashing against the foot of a cliff can do considerable damage.

Cliffs made of soft rocks stand little chance against fierce waves, and they simply crumble away. Some low cliffs can be worn back by more than a metre during just one storm.

But even cliffs made from hard rocks can be weakened and eventually destroyed by waves.

▼ ① **When waves break against a cliff, the force of the water is like a hammer beating on the rock (A). When the wave is spent, any loosened blocks can fall out (B). Then the next wave approaches, hammering the cliff once more (C). (Note: it may take many years for waves to prise a block loose.)**

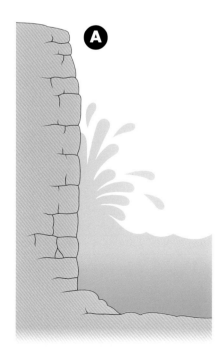

A

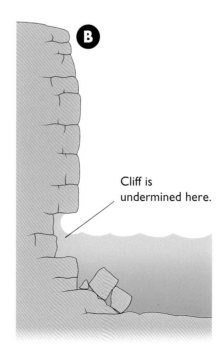

B

Cliff is undermined here.

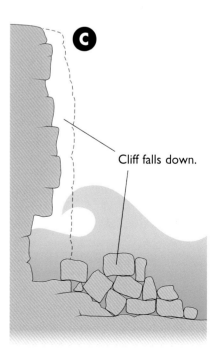

C

Cliff falls down.

Breaking waves

As a wave approaches a cliff, the front of the wave rears up to form a curved, foaming top, or **BREAKER**. The breaker moves forward with great speed, throwing tonnes of foaming water against the <u>bottom</u> of the cliff (picture ①).

Water and air bubbles are forced into even the tiniest of cracks in the rock. As the main part of the wave crashes onto the cliff, the air and water in the cracks is squashed, and this is like driving a wedge into the cracks.

Once the wave has broken, it collapses, and the water and air in the cracks rush out again. Then, within a few seconds, a new breaker arrives and the process happens all over again.

In time, this repeated pounding action begins to loosen blocks of rock, and they fall into the sea. This leaves the upper part of the cliff overhanging.

When the overhang becomes large, the upper part of the cliff collapses (picture ②).

So, by simply breaking against the bottom of the cliff, the waves cause the whole cliff to wear back.

▼ ② **Waves attack the bottom of a cliff in southern Australia, wearing it away. From time to time, the cliff becomes so undermined that it simply collapses. (Because rockfalls of this kind can happen without warning, it is unsafe to go near the foot of tall cliffs.)**

13

Wearing cliffs away

Many waves lift sand and pebbles and throw them against the cliffs. The effect of this is to scrape the rock away like natural sandpaper.

Just the sheer weight of moving water can reduce a cliff to rubble, as we saw on pages 12 and 13. But most waves are not simply water – they also carry sand and pebbles that they have picked up from the sea bed (picture ①).

As waves crash against the foot of a cliff, so the sand and pebbles caught up in the water batter the cliff and knock little pieces off. At the same time the sand and pebbles are broken up and made smaller and more rounded. This sandpaper-like action is called **ABRASION**.

Cliff notch

You can see the force of abrasion in the smooth groove, or notch, near the foot of a cliff (picture ②). On the beach in front of it will lie the pebbles and sand that are picked up by the waves and thrown at the cliff during storms (picture ③).

▼ ① **All of these stones were once parts of rocky cliffs. Once plucked from the cliffs they were thrown back at the cliffs by storm waves. This helped to scour away the cliff and, at the same time, made the stones smaller and more rounded.**

These large stones are called pebbles.

These smaller pieces are gravel. They are pebbles that have been broken up as they crashed against the waves.

These finer pieces are sand. They are the smallest grains on a beach. They too are the result of the crashing action of waves.

When a **WAVE-CUT NOTCH** becomes too deep, the top of the cliff above will fall down. In this way, the whole cliff is eroded when the bottom of the cliff is worn away.

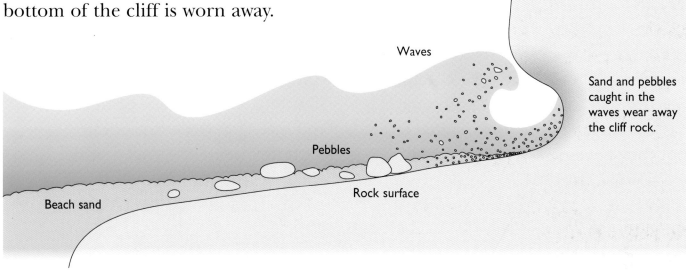

Waves

Sand and pebbles caught in the waves wear away the cliff rock.

Pebbles

Rock surface

Beach sand

▲ ② This diagram shows how the waves throw sand and pebbles at the cliff and wear a notch in it.

▼ ③ Waves, armed with pebbles, have scoured out this smooth-shaped notch at the foot of a white chalk cliff near Durdle Dor in Dorset.

Why cliffs are different shapes

The shape of a cliff depends on the kind of rocks that it is made from. Strong rocks give upright cliffs, while weak rocks give sloping cliffs. A mixture of hard and soft rocks gives cliffs that look like natural staircases.

The shape of a coast is made varied by the cliffs. Some cliffs are tall and rise vertically from the sea. Others are like natural staircases, while yet others are hummocky and gentle.

This variety in cliffs is not caused by the way the waves work, but by the kind of rock in the cliff.

Strong rock cliffs

Cliffs of strong rocks are usually tall and upright (picture ①). The rocks behave like a wall, falling down only very occasionally when waves cut far enough into the bottom of the cliff.

Weak rock cliffs

Cliffs made of weak rocks cannot stand up to the attack of the sea (picture ②). Because they are naturally weak, the rocks easily collapse and give frequent **LANDSLIDES** and **MUDFLOWS**.

Natural staircase cliffs

Where hard and soft rocks lie in layers one on top of another, the hard rocks control the shape of the cliff (picture ③). You can see that the hard layers wear away less easily than the soft layers because they make the ledges that stand out of the cliff face.

◀▼ ① This is Beachy Head, East Sussex, one of the tallest cliffs in the UK. The rock is chalk.

▼ ② When a cliff is made from soft rocks, the rock cannot stand vertically and it frequently collapses. This may result in a landslide, as shown in this example from Devon. Cliffs liable to landslides are hummocky and often covered in scrubby plants (as shown on the left of the picture). Compare this with the harder rock that makes the vertical cliffs on the right of the picture.

▼ ③ When layers of hard and soft rock occur in a cliff, you get a shape like a staircase. The hard rock layers take longer to wear away than the soft layers and so they stand out as ledges. The ledges finally break off when enough of the soft rock below them has fallen away. This cliff is at Whitby, North Yorkshire.

Hard rock layer

Soft rock layer

17

Caves, arches and stacks

As cliffs are worn back, the softer rocks are scooped out to make caves, leaving harder rocks as arches and sea stacks.

Waves can pick out weaknesses in rocks that are difficult to see. This is why a cliff may look as though it is made of the same rock, but be worn away only in some places and not others.

You can tell where rocks have areas of weakness from the occurrence of deep narrow inlets (also called **COVES**), **CAVES** (picture ①), natural **ARCHES** and pillars of rock called **STACKS** standing in the sea (picture ②).

Cave

Sea caves are deep, natural hollows or tunnels in a cliff. They are formed when waves pound on a band of weaker rock. This means that the weak rock can be worked away faster than its surroundings.

Sea caves can form in any rock that is strong enough to support a cave roof without it collapsing.

Holes, known as **BLOWHOLES**, may eventually be forced through the roof of the cave. Once this occurs, the pressure created by each wave is released through the blowhole as a jet of spray.

Arch

As caves become deeper, there is a chance they may break right through a headland. When this happens, they make a natural stone arch (see the picture on page 1).

◄ ① Caves can tell you a lot about which rocks are soft, how thick the rocks are and in which direction they are sloping.

The cave shown here in silhouette 'leans' to the right because this is the way the soft rocks slope. The cave in the distance has a similar shape. Both caves have been eroded from the same band of soft rock. The width of the cave tells you the thickness of the soft band of rock.

Stack

The roof of the arch gradually gets worn higher and wider. Eventually the top of the arch collapses and leaves one wall of the arch standing on its own in the sea. This pillar of rock is called a **STACK**, a needle if it is very thin, and a stump if it is mostly worn down (picture ③).

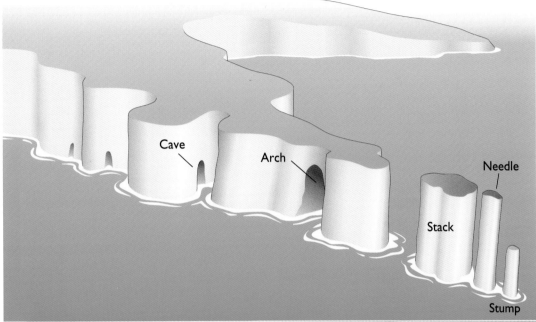

Cave

Arch

Needle

Stack

Stump

◄ ② The main features of a headland are stacks, needles, stumps, arches and caves.

▼ ③ These are the caves and stacks of 'Old Harry and his wives', Dorset.

Estuaries, lochs and fjords

If the sea rises, or the land sinks, it can flood the coast. A flooded lowland valley is called an estuary. A flooded valley within mountains is called a fjord, sea loch or sound.

Over the centuries, sea levels and land levels change. If the land sinks, or the sea level rises, then many coastlines will be drowned.

It is easier to work out what a drowned coast looks like if you think about a valley that has recently been used for a reservoir. Here, the water level has risen quickly, so the valley sides dip straight down into the water. There has been no time for waves to cut cliffs and there is no beach on which waves can lap.

Most drowned valleys are the result of how sea levels changed during the **ICE AGE** (picture ①).

▶ ① These diagrams shows how lochs, fjords and estuaries are formed during ice ages.
(A) What the coast looked like before the Ice Age.
(B) During the Ice Age, the water from the sea is stored as ice on land and the sea level falls. Glaciers and rivers cut deeply into the newly exposed sea bed on their way to the new shore.
(C) At the end of the Ice Age, the ice melts and becomes sea water again. The sea level rises and floods into the deepened valleys, drowning their lower parts. Lochs and estuaries are formed.

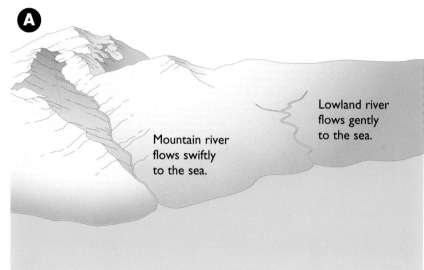

A

Mountain river flows swiftly to the sea.

Lowland river flows gently to the sea.

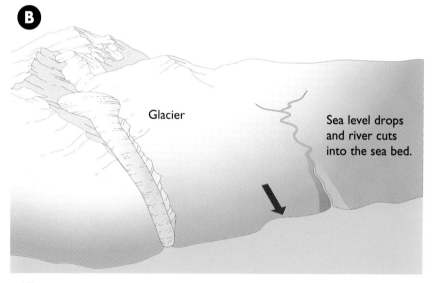

B

Glacier

Sea level drops and river cuts into the sea bed.

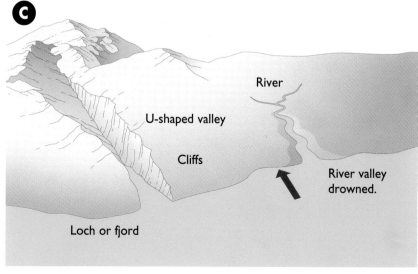

C

River

U-shaped valley

Cliffs

River valley drowned.

Loch or fjord

Drowned valleys

Drowned coastal valleys are given special names. If the valley was wide and shallow, and is part of a lowland area, then it is called an **ESTUARY**. If the valley was cut by a glacier, and is in a mountain area, it is called a **SEA LOCH** in Scotland. Other names used around the world include **FJORD** (Norway) and **SOUND** (Canada, New Zealand and the United States).

Drowned valleys may stretch inland for many kilometres, so that the tides reach tens, or even hundreds, of kilometres inland.

Many big port cities have been founded on the sheltered banks of estuaries, taking advantage of the deep water that occurs in all drowned valleys. London, New York, San Francisco and Sydney are just some of the many examples of port cities built on estuaries.

A drowned glacial valley (picture ②) has very steep sides, so there is no place for cities to be built and they tend to remain areas of wilderness.

▼ ② **If you see a valley where the sides plunge straight into the water, then it is probably a drowned valley. Milford Sound, South Island, New Zealand, is a fjord, cut by a glacier and now flooded by the sea. Fjords are often over 600 metres deep.**

Waves on the beach

When waves approach a beach they rear up and then break, sending foaming water and sand first up, and then down, the beach.

Breaking waves, or **BREAKERS,** are important because they move sand about on a beach.

Winds push waves towards the shore in long, rolling lines. Close to the shore, where the water becomes shallow, the waves get taller, and the tops curve over and form breakers of white, foamy water (picture ① and ②).

Breakers

Once a wave has broken, it rushes onshore in a mass of foam. This foaming water is called **SURF**, and the surf that moves up the beach is called **SWASH**.

Eventually, the water cannot push forward any more. Some water sinks into the sand,

▼ ① These two pictures show how a wave breaks. On the left, you can see the breaker plunging down onto the beach. On the right, you can see the foamy surf (called swash) churning about a few moments later.

▼ ② As waves move onto the beach, they curve over and then break, to give a mass of foam. The red arrows show how sand is dug out of the beach each time a wave breaks.

while the rest starts to flow back down the beach. This part of the surf is called **BACKWASH**.

Usually the swash of one wave crashes into the backwash of the wave before it. You can see the way this happens in pictures ③ **A–D**.

The sand you cannot see

If you were to stand in the surf on a beach, you would see the surf, but your toes would feel the push and pull of the water, and the movement of sand. Breaking waves move some sand about, even on a calm day.

Fine weather, stormy weather

The pictures on this page were all taken in fine weather, when the waves are small and bathing is safe. During a storm, the wind blows more strongly, and the waves grow taller and crash more fiercely onto the beach. At these times the swash and backwash are powerful enough to move huge amounts of sand backwards and forwards up the beach. On the next pages you will see how important this movement is.

◀ ③ In picture A, people are waiting for the next wave to run up the beach. A breaker has just formed. Notice that the backwash from the last wave is still flowing off the beach. It is shown to the right of the bathers. Notice, also, the wake around their feet.

In picture B, the new wave is breaking.

In picture C, the surf (swash) is pushing up the beach, mixing with the water still running back down the beach.

In picture D, the swash has gone as far up the beach as it can. At the same time, a new wave is breaking.

⚠ Do not go near the surf without a responsible adult in attendance.

Sand and shingle beaches

Some beaches are covered in marvellous fine sand. But others are muddy and some are made entirely of pebbles. It all depends on the waves.

A **BEACH** is a strip of land washed over each day by the tides. Beaches are mainly found in bays (picture ①).

Most beaches are sandy, but some are pebbly. Pebbly beaches are called **SHINGLE** beaches. A few beaches are gravelly.

Most beaches are made of pieces of rock that have been worn from cliffs. The colour of these beaches is normally similar to the nearby rocks. Some beaches in the tropics are made only of broken sea shells and coral. These are pure white. Some beaches

▲▼ ① A beach is mostly made of sand or pebbles. But you can also find many other materials, such as fragments of sea shells. This is because many creatures make the beach their home. Waves carrying pebbles smash shells into small fragments. For this reason, shells survive best on sandy beaches.

The way beach materials are sorted is shown on the diagram below.

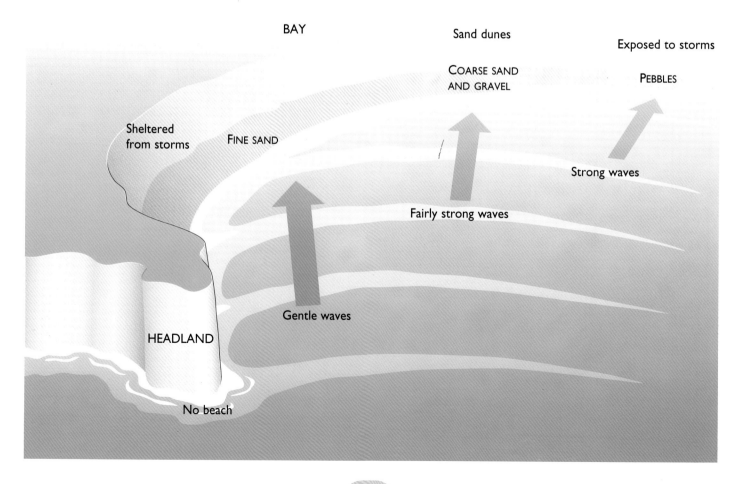

BAY

Sand dunes

Exposed to storms

COARSE SAND AND GRAVEL

PEBBLES

Sheltered from storms

FINE SAND

Strong waves

Fairly strong waves

Gentle waves

HEADLAND

No beach

◀ ② This is a beach made of pebbles. Pebbly beaches are often very steep. This can make them unattractive for holidaymakers.

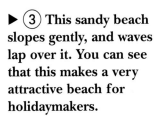

▶ ③ This sandy beach slopes gently, and waves lap over it. You can see that this makes a very attractive beach for holidaymakers.

are made of lava from volcanoes. These beaches are black.

Steep beaches are made of shingle

Waves easily sort out the various sizes of material. Wherever the coast faces storm winds, the waves are sometimes fierce, so mud and sand cannot settle – only pebbles are heavy enough not be swept back out to sea. Pebbles always make steep beaches (picture ②).

Gently sloping beaches are made of sand

Waves cannot bring pebbles to parts of the beach that are sheltered, such as in bays (picture ③). In these places, beaches are made of sand and are gently sloping (but not flat).

Flat beaches are made of mud

Even MUD can settle in very sheltered places such as near estuaries. Muddy beaches are almost flat, but the sticky mud is not very attractive to walk on.

Beaches of many uses

Some parts of a beach are used by holidaymakers more than others. This is why.

During summer, a sandy beach can become filled with holidaymakers. Such a large number of people can have a very big impact on the beach and the features around it, but the beach also has an impact on them.

Choosing a spot on the beach

Look closely at picture ① and you will see that people are not scattered evenly over the beach, but are crowded together. This happens because some parts of the beach are more suitable to use than others.

The top of the beach

The top of the beach (picture ②) is the highest and driest part of the beach. It is out of reach of the waves for the longest part of each day, and it is the most sheltered part of the beach. For all of these reasons, many people choose this part of the beach to sit or sunbathe on, and so it becomes the most crowded.

▼ ① Holidaymakers make use of the dry upper beach at the most sheltered end of a bay. This is Woolacombe in Devon.

▼ ② **There are actually many parts to a beach.**

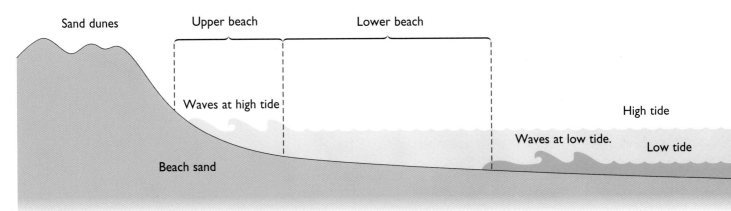

Sand dunes   Upper beach   Lower beach

Waves at high tide

High tide

Waves at low tide.

Low tide

Beach sand

The bottom of the beach

This is the part that is closest to the sea. It is uncovered for only a short time. It is also nearly flat. This means that, even when the tide is out, water is only just below the surface. It is also a very windswept place. People may play games on this part of the beach, because there are fewer people about, but they do not usually want to sit on the cold, wet sand.

The low part of the beach often contains wavy ridges – called **RIPPLES** – made by waves as they move over flat sand.

The back of the beach

If a wind blows onshore at low tide, it will carry sand from the beach onto the land. Here it may be trapped by plants. In this way, hills of sand called **SAND DUNES** build up in the middle of many bays (picture ③).

Sand dunes make good, sheltered, sunbathing spots, although the tough grass is uncomfortable to sit on.

Plants growing in sand dunes are easily killed if they are frequently trampled on.

▼ ③ **Coastal sand dunes give good protection to the land close to the shore. If the plants are killed, the sand is more easily blown about and the dunes may be lost. This is why dunes need to be fenced off to protect the plants if there are many holidaymakers about.**

Weblink:www.CurriculumVisions.com/coast

Moving sand

Waves rarely break straight onto a beach, but are usually at an angle. This is what causes sand to move along the beach – and even build new beaches.

When you stand in the surf, you notice the way the water moves up and down. But look again and you will see that most waves do not go straight up the beach, but instead move up at an angle (picture ①).

You can see this most easily if you drop something that floats on the surf. After a few breakers have run up the beach, you will see that the float has not been washed up onto the beach, nor been washed out to sea, but has <u>drifted</u> sideways <u>along the shore</u> (picture ②).

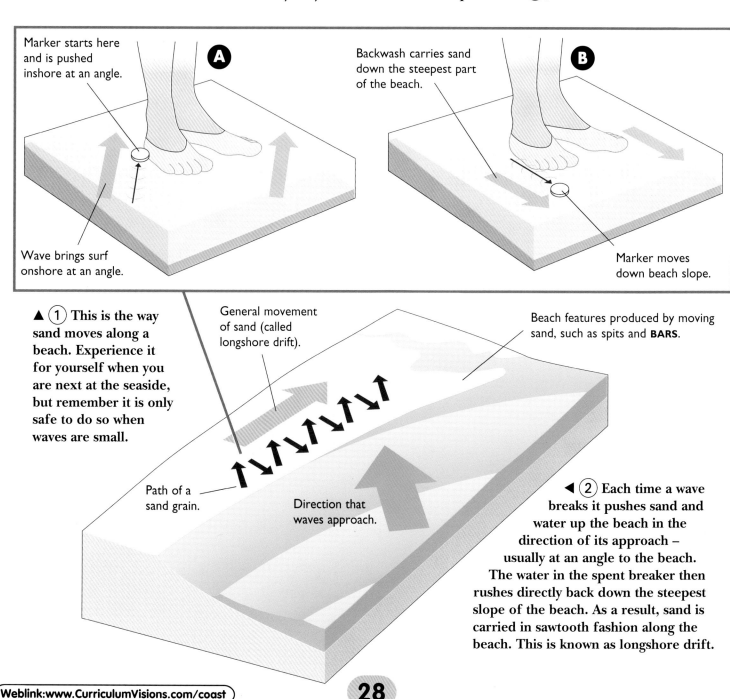

A

Marker starts here and is pushed inshore at an angle.

Wave brings surf onshore at an angle.

B

Backwash carries sand down the steepest part of the beach.

Marker moves down beach slope.

▲ ① This is the way sand moves along a beach. Experience it for yourself when you are next at the seaside, but remember it is only safe to do so when waves are small.

General movement of sand (called longshore drift).

Beach features produced by moving sand, such as spits and **BARS**.

Path of a sand grain.

Direction that waves approach.

◀ ② Each time a wave breaks it pushes sand and water up the beach in the direction of its approach – usually at an angle to the beach. The water in the spent breaker then rushes directly back down the steepest slope of the beach. As a result, sand is carried in sawtooth fashion along the beach. This is known as longshore drift.

How to spot sand on the move

There are many features on the beach that show you how sand nearly always moves in the same direction. The movement of sand along a beach is called TRANSPORT. Some kinds of transport are natural, and some are man-made. Natural transport is called LONGSHORE DRIFT.

Picture ③ shows a beach from the air. A lot of sand (brown colour) is being churned up by the water. You can see how the waves are pushing it to the left.

Picture ④ shows a new beach built across a bay by the settling out, or DEPOSITING, of drifting sand caught in the waves.

Drifting sand can cause problems for seaside resorts, and they often try to trap the sand by building fences – called GROYNES – in the beach (see also page 37). These fences are ideal for spotting the direction of drift (picture ⑤). The sand will be piled up against the side it is being carried toward.

When drift works

Waves will carry sand all year long. Big pebbles will only be carried during storms.

Sand and pebbles drift in the same direction as the wind blows. So, if the wind blows from the southwest for most of the year, the sand will drift, on average, towards the northeast, and so on.

▲ ③ From the air you can more easily see sand being carried along by waves and currents. Notice that, although the land has changed direction, the waves and sand have not. As the waves carry the sand into deeper water, it settles out. Where the sand settles, a new beach begins to form. This is Santa Monica, California.

▲ ④ A beach almost closing off an estuary. This kind of long beach is called a SAND SPIT. This example is Stinson Beach, California.

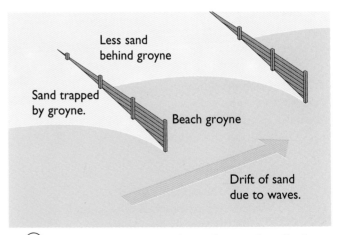

▲ ⑤ Beach fences (groynes) can be used to find out the direction in which beach sand is drifting.

Deltas

A delta is a place where material carried by a river is laid down in the sea.

The coast gets much of its sand, silt and mud by wearing away cliffs. But lots of sand, silt and mud are also brought to the sea by rivers.

When a river brings more material than the sea can wash away, the material starts to build up and forms a DELTA.

Fan-shaped deltas

There are two common shapes of delta. One shape is like a fan (picture ①). It has many channels that spread out evenly from the main river. As a result, the sand and silt are laid down evenly around the edge of the delta and it has a smooth shape (picture ②).

Bird's foot deltas

The other kind of delta is produced when a river has only a small number of channels (picture ③). It resembles the shape of the claws on a bird's foot and as a result is called a bird's foot delta. The Mississippi delta (picture ④) is an example of a bird's foot delta.

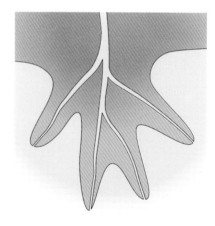

◄ ③ Bird's-foot delta. This kind of delta forms when a single main channel changes direction frequently.

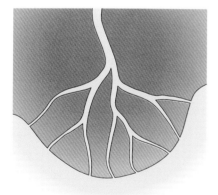

▲ ① Fan-shaped delta. This kind of delta forms wherever channels spread out evenly across the delta.

► ② This is the fan delta of the River Niger in West Africa. It reaches the sea in Nigeria. Notice the mainly small channels spread out evenly across it. This is why the edge of the delta is so even.

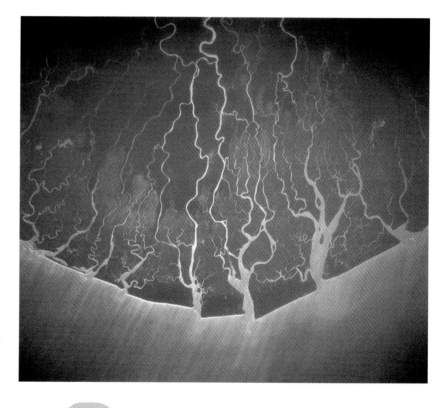

Deltas make new land

As new material is laid down by rivers entering the sea, so deltas grow out from the coast and make new land. Some countries, such as Bangladesh in Asia, and the Netherlands in Europe, lie entirely on deltas.

Only the world's biggest rivers can create long-lasting deltas, because otherwise the currents and waves of the sea would wash them away.

Deltas are not very common in the UK because most rivers enter the sea in estuaries (see page 20). Deltas will only grow from the British coast when the estuaries have been filled in.

◀▲ ④ **This is the Mississippi delta on the coast of the Gulf of Mexico. The Mississippi is North America's largest river, and you can see it winding towards the sea in these pictures. The delta is everything that stretches beyond the normal coastline. Look for the plume of sand and silt off the end of the delta. It is being pushed in one direction by the sea currents.**

(Note: you will find further information on deltas in The River Book in the Curriculum Visions series).

Weblink:www.CurriculumVisions.com/coast

Living on crumbling cliffs

Many cliffs are made of soft rock which continually tumbles into the sea. It is not a good place to build on.

A cliff forms because the sea has cut into the land. Wherever you see a cliff you know the cliff is wearing back, or eroding (picture ①).

Although all cliffs erode, some erode faster than others. Cliffs made of the same rock, that face directly into storm winds, will wear away faster than rock that is sheltered. Cliffs made of soft rocks will erode much more quickly than those made from hard rocks.

Low cliffs will always wear away faster than tall cliffs of the same rock, simply because there is less rock for the sea to erode.

The cliffs that wear away fastest are therefore low cliffs made of soft rock that stand in the full force of storm winds (picture ②).

Building near cliffs

It is always risky to build close to the coast, but especially so where the cliffs are made of soft rock. As waves attack these cliffs, they cause **LANDSLIDES** that take huge bites out of the cliff (picture ② and ③).

▼ ① These cliffs in Hawaii give attractive views over the sea but they are made of soft rock which is retreating quickly. You can see this by looking at the buildings closest to the sea. Notice what is happening to car parks, tennis courts and so on.

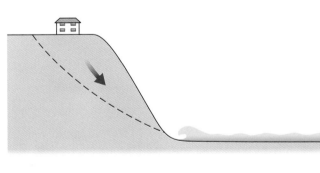

◄▲ ② Thick, soft rocks cannot stand up at steep angles. So when the sea cuts away at the bottom of a soft-rock cliff, it will begin to collapse. Collapse usually happens after heavy rain, when the rock has soaked up water. The water makes it easier for the rock to slide.

Here you can see what happened to part of the Holbeck Hotel, Scarborough, North Yorkshire in June 1993. The soft rock beneath it simply slipped onto the beach.

Notice that the cliff is very scarred, showing that parts of the cliff slide quite frequently.

▶ ③ This cliff in Christchurch, Hampshire, is eroding rapidly. In this photograph, you can see whole slabs of the cliff have recently slipped.

Weblink:www.CurriculumVisions.com/coast

Living by a stormy beach

Living by the beach has many attractions, but it can also bring dangers when storm waves are about.

In the past, most people built their homes in sheltered estuaries away from the fierce winter storms (picture ①).

Today, more people want to live beside the seaside, and many want to live right next to the beach. But although this can be safe, in general the rule is: the closer you are to the sea, the more dangerous it is.

Beaches and islands

Beaches and low-lying coastal islands are made of sand (picture ②). They were built by waves, and can easily be reshaped by waves. People who live on sandy islands therefore put themselves at risk.

Stormy seas are much higher than normal seas, so floods, as well as waves, become a real danger for people living close to beaches (picture ③). When storm winds blow, the level of the sea is much higher than normal. Furthermore, the waves can pick up and carry stones. A combination of high tide, storm waves and crashing pebbles can be terrifyingly destructive.

▲ ① This is what living beside the sea used to mean: a sheltered harbour out of the direct line of storms (Staithes, North Yorkshire).

▶ ② It is very attractive to live beside the sea, with the beach outside your front door. But in stormy weather this is a very dangerous place to be. When storm waves batter houses, stones are thrown against buildings and sea levels rise, causing floods. If the sand is washed away, the buildings may lose all of their foundations and collapse. The weather map shows a hurricane off the coast of the United States.

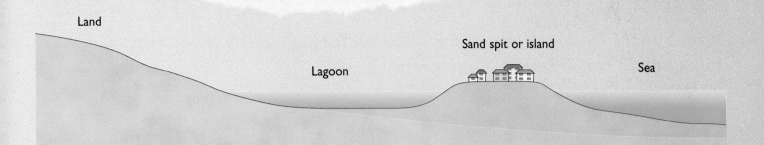

Land

Sand spit or island

Lagoon

Sea

▲ ③ Low islands are favourite places for holiday houses. The more expensive homes look towards the sea, while the less expensive homes look inland across the lagoon. In this case, the more expensive homes are in the greatest danger.

You can find BARRIER ISLANDS and holiday homes along the entire 'hurricane coast' of east and south USA.

Dangers by the beach

Some people believe in living right on the beach (picture ④). To do this, their homes have to be built on stilts. Twice a day, as the tide comes in, the houses are literally in the sea. This kind of beach-side living is definitely risky.

◀▶ ④ This is what living right at the beach can mean: threatened by storm waves in front and cliff collapse behind! This is Santa Monica, California.

Storm waves

Storm sea level

Normal waves

Normal sea level

Protecting yourself from the sea

Sea defences can protect people living on the coast – at least for a while. But they can be both ugly and expensive.

The coast is one of the most densely settled parts of many countries. People prefer to build their houses facing the sea. But, as we have seen, in many places the sea is continually eroding the land. Where the rocks are soft, erosion is fast, and people are often in danger of losing their homes.

To prevent the loss of homes, sea walls and other types of SEA DEFENCES are built (picture ①).

Sea walls

When people think of sea defences, they often think of SEA WALLS. A sea wall is built to take the full force of storm waves and protect people living behind it. Sea walls are very expensive to build. Unfortunately, no matter how much money is spent, it is difficult to build a sea wall that can stand up to the fiercest of the waves, so walls have to be rebuilt time after time (picture ②).

Beach fences

If you look at many coastal areas with wide beaches, you will see fences running out to sea. These fences are called groynes (see page 29 and picture ③). They are there

▼ ② Storm waves breaking over a sea wall.

▲ ① Sea walls and groynes have been built at the bottom of many cliffs.

▼ ③ At Selsey, West Sussex, groynes have been built across a beach. They are designed to make sure the wide beach stays in place and so waves do not reach the houses close to the shore.

to hold the sand in place and make the beach wider. When the beach is wide enough, even monster waves will rarely reach the land and waves will break up on the beach.

Groynes are much cheaper to build than sea walls, which is why they are so commonly used along coasts where erosion is a problem.

Cliff-foot boulders

Scientists have found better ways of protecting a cliff than a sea wall or groynes. One popular (and cheap) way is to use piles of boulders dumped at the foot of a cliff. Waves crash on the boulders and use up their energy, so there is not enough energy left for erosion. The boulders have to be big – otherwise they will be carried away by the waves (picture ④). This is a sustainable form of development (see page 38).

◄ ④ Boulders are very effective. But the size of the boulders makes them difficult to walk across, so they are not used much in holiday resorts. This is California.

How should we use the coast?

Even if people don't build sea walls or other defences, the coastal environment can still be under threat from too much development.

The seaside is a very attractive place to be. As more people get longer holidays or retire earlier from work, these people want to be by the seaside.

In the future, you could imagine that our entire coast might be lined with houses and hotels. If this is not the future we want, then we have to plan to stop it now.

However, it can be difficult to satisfy everyone's needs, as you can see in the points of view shown on these pages. What we want to do is to manage the coast for our own use, and for the benefit of nature. This is called **STEWARDSHIP**. The type of changes we make must not wreck the coast. This is called **SUSTAINABLE DEVELOPMENT**.

☞ The hotel owner's point of view:
"I want to build a hotel for all the people who want to have a holiday by the sea. But of course I also want to build steps down the cliff and have a piece of private beach. After all, my customers are paying for their seaside holiday."

☞ The day-tripper's point of view:
"I want to be able to park my car on the cliff top and then get down to the beach where I can sunbathe all day. I also want toilets and cafes nearby so I don't have to go far from the beach.
I havn't given much thought to conservation. I just want to enjoy my sunbathing."

▼ This is Blackpool, Britain's most famous beach. But the points of view shown here could be for any coastal resort in the world.

☞ The retired couple's point of view:
"We have saved up all our working lives and now we want to retire by the sea. We don't want a house a kilometre from the sea – we want a house by the sea."

☞ The rambler's point of view:
"I want to enjoy all the coastal views and follow a coastal footpath. I want everyone to be able to walk along the coast. I don't think it is right that any of it should be private land. The coast belongs to all of the people in the country, not just a rich few."

☞ The builder's point of view:
"I have lots of customers who want houses and have the money to buy them. I don't see that the coast is any different. I just want a strip along the sea front, that's all."

☞ The conservationist's point of view:
"This coast is home to millions of wild creatures. Birds nest on the cliffs and beaches, and rare plants grow there, too. They have a right to live. It is important to conserve the coast and keep it natural and wild. It is also important to make some parts of it difficult to get to. This will mean that it is quiet and birds and other animals aren't frightened off."

Weblink:www.curriculumvisions.com/coast

Learning to leave the coast alone

Sea defences are always unsightly and often expensive. But it is possible to work with nature and not against it – and it costs nothing.

The coast is one of the most rapidly changing parts of the environment. Many countries spend large amounts of money on 'defending' their coasts. This is money they would not have to spend if they worked with the coast instead of against it.

Understand that coasts will always erode

Coastal waves work like this (picture ①):

- Waves erode some parts of the coast. This produces sand.

- The waves carry the sand along the coast. This uses up energy so the waves don't erode these parts of the coast very much.

- The sand finally settles out and makes **SANDBANKS**. The waves don't erode this part of the coast at all.

If you stop the waves eroding naturally, you will upset the way the coast works, and the waves will simply erode somewhere else. Protecting one place usually puts another place in danger.

▼ ① **You can decide where and where not to build by finding out first what the waves are doing.**

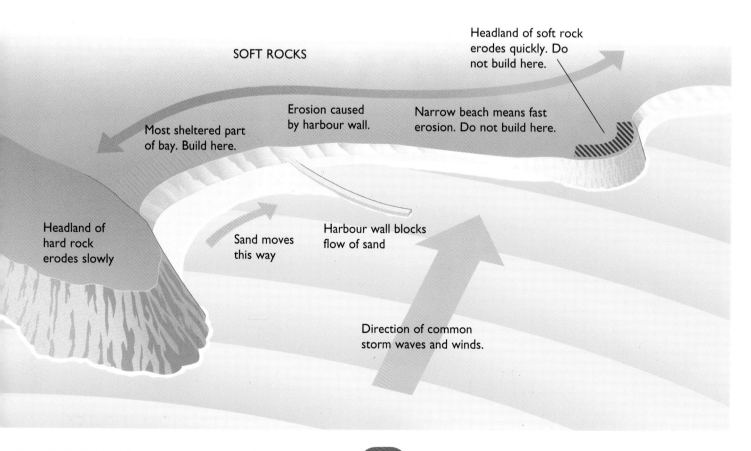

SOFT ROCKS

Headland of soft rock erodes quickly. Do not build here.

Most sheltered part of bay. Build here.

Erosion caused by harbour wall.

Narrow beach means fast erosion. Do not build here.

Headland of hard rock erodes slowly

Sand moves this way

Harbour wall blocks flow of sand

Direction of common storm waves and winds.

Look to see where the waves are eroding

It is easy to find out what the waves are doing. Look to see where cliffs show fresh signs of wear. Where this happens, the waves have lots of energy to erode the cliffs. It makes sense not to build where the cliffs erode quickly.

Storm waves will always erode soft rocks faster than hard rocks. Low cliffs will always erode faster than high cliffs. It makes sense not to build in places facing storm waves unless the cliff rock is hard.

Look to see where new sand is settling out

When waves carry sand from place to place they use up energy. If they use energy carrying sand, they cannot use that energy to erode cliffs. This is why a wide beach is a good protection against erosion. If the sand is settling out to make sandbanks and low islands, the land behind them (not on them) will be naturally protected and a safe place to build houses.

Think about the future

We may not be able to do much about houses that have already been built in hazardous places. But we can stop people making the same mistakes in the future (picture ②). This is where planners come in. They can stop any future building close to retreating coasts, and encourage people to build where the sand is settling out. This saves property being damaged and costs absolutely nothing.

▼ ② **The coast near Lisbon, Portugal. Compare the developments with those shown in Picture 1.**

Beach pollution

There are many ways that beaches can become polluted. The most dangerous pollution is the waste that we pour into the sea each day, and oil spills.

As the waves rise and fall each day, they wash the beach clean – or at least that is what we expect. But although the sea is very good at cleaning the beach, there are times and places where it simply can't cope.

In fact, for hundreds of years people have supposed that anything they put in the sea will be carried away. So they have dumped all their waste in the sea and forgotten about it. However, as more people now live by the sea, the amount of waste poured or pumped into the sea has increased greatly.

Pollution that returns to kill

If you look at almost any beach you will find waste materials – **FLOTSAM** – washed up onto it (picture ①). Flotsam shows how many of the things we dump into the sea are

simply carried back onto the beach by the waves and currents.

In many parts of the world, coastal towns and cities pour their sewage through pipes directly into the sea (picture ②). But, as we have seen earlier in this book, waves can push water back onto the beach, so it is possible for all the sewage to be

▲ ① Typical flotsam on the beach. What you can see may be dangerous. But the water may also contains dangerous germs you can't see.

▶ ② Estuaries and coastal inlets are most at risk because the water is not stirred up much and so does not clean itself very quickly. These are also the places where most people live. This map shows how disasters can occur. The sewage pipe for a town leads out to sea, well clear of the town. Nevertheless, the waves and currents simply drive the sewage back to the town's beach and into the estuary.

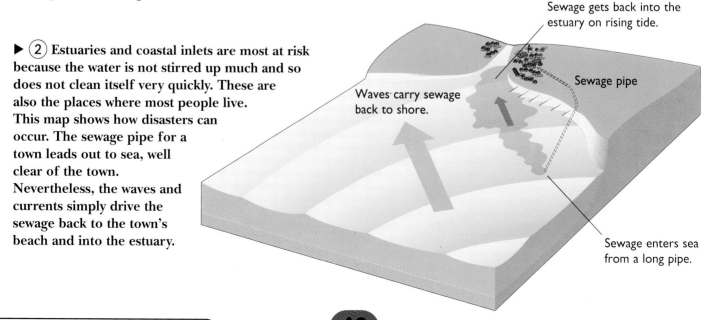

Sewage gets back into the estuary on rising tide.

Sewage pipe

Waves carry sewage back to shore.

Sewage enters sea from a long pipe.

washed back up on the beach. The difference is that, while you can see the floating waste, you cannot see the germs that have also been washed back up onto the beach.

Oil pollution

One of the greatest dangers to beaches, and ocean wildlife, is pollution by oil. If a ship releases oil at sea, or a storm pushes a ship against rocks or on a beach and damages it, then millions of litres of oil can be released (picture ③).

Some oil floats and makes a film called an **OIL SLICK**. An oil slick seals

▼ ③ When a pipeline or an oil tanker is holed, the waves carry some of the oil on the surface, while currents carry other parts across the sea bed. As a result, oil pollution is very difficult to deal with. These wrecked ships lie along the coast of Madagascar.

the water so that no air can get into it. This can kill beach life. When birds wade in the water, or swim on the surface, they get covered with oil. As they hunt for food in the sand, they eat the oil. Oil is a poison. Many birds and countless creatures living in the beach sand may die when there is an oil spill.

Some oil forms into tar balls. It sinks to the bottom and is then rolled back and forth by the waves. Tar balls may wash up on beaches for months or years after a spill.

Cleaning up

When a disaster happens, many people try their best to collect and clean up the beach and rocks, and to rescue and clean the wildlife. But most wildlife caught in an oil spill still dies.

Beach

Ship holed

Oil slick

Tar balls

Oil slicks cause a lot of damage, and are very expensive to clean up. This is the 1989 Exxon Valdez accident, Alaska.

Wildlife at the coast

We are not alone in living by the sea. Millions of plants and animals use it as their home, too.

The coast is one of the most densely populated parts of the world – by wildlife. So when we go to live by the coast, we need to keep the needs of wildlife in mind as well.

Hiding in the beach

When the tide goes out the beach may look empty and lifeless. But this is because the creatures that live on the beach are sea animals. At low tide, they hide in burrows in the sand of beaches (picture ①) and in the mud in estuaries.

Making the most of the surf

Wherever a wave breaks, the sand is disturbed, and small animals that live just below the sand surface can be tossed into the water and more easily be caught by birds (picture ②).

Living in rock pools

Rock pools are bowl-shaped hollows which hold sea water when the tide goes out (picture ③).

A rock pool is a very difficult place to live in, because of the constantly changing level of the tide and the battering by the waves. Clearly, a rock pool is no place for large living things, or those that are in any way delicate.

Animals like crabs, shrimps and small fish take shelter from waves under rocky ledges or stones. Some can burrow into the sandy bottom of the pool.

▶ ② **A wading bird probes for food in the surf using its long beak.**

▼ ① **Animals are exposed on the open sandy surface of a beach, so they often bury themselves to escape predators.**

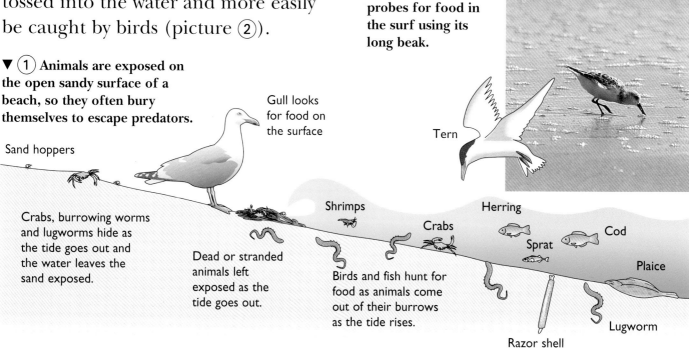

Sand hoppers

Gull looks for food on the surface

Crabs, burrowing worms and lugworms hide as the tide goes out and the water leaves the sand exposed.

Dead or stranded animals left exposed as the tide goes out.

Shrimps

Crabs

Birds and fish hunt for food as animals come out of their burrows as the tide rises.

Herring

Sprat

Cod

Plaice

Razor shell

Lugworm

Tern

▼ ③ Rock pools contain a great variety of animals and plants that are well adapted to a difficult environment.

The oyster-catcher has a chisel-shaped bill, to open limpets and other shells, or to prise them off rocks.

Limpets have streamlined shells so they are not easily pulled off the rock by breaking waves. Their shells are thick, so they do not crack easily if they are hit by pebbles in the waves.

The sea anemone closes up tight during low tide. It only opens when the sea rises – then it sends out stinging tentacles.

The flexible, waving fronds of seaweeds move with the waves and so are not broken by them.

Starfish can use suction cups to hang onto the rocky surface of the pool while waves are breaking.

Tiny algae that float in the sea water are the food for many animals, such as limpets and mussels.

A blenny is a typical small rockpool fish. It has eyes on top of its head, so that it can spot a bird trying to stab it from above. Its mottled colours help to camouflage it among the pebbles at the bottom of the rock pool.

Hermit crabs eat food that gets washed in by waves.

Finding a home on the cliffs

The sea contains a huge amount of food, and this is why so many birds make their homes by the coast (picture ④).

Many of the most noticeable sea birds nest in colonies on tall cliffs, where they build their nests on ledges. Not only are they close to their food supplies here, but their eggs and chicks are more easily protected both from other wild animals and people.

Preserving wildlife

Wildlife is most affected when their food and homes are polluted by oil and sewage. But when we build on cliffs, nesting grounds can also be lost. This is one reason we need to leave large tracts of coast undisturbed.

▼ ④ Seabirds use ledges on cliffs as nesting sites.

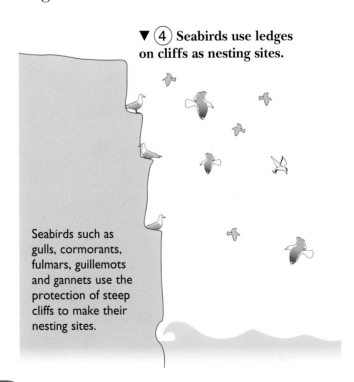

Seabirds such as gulls, cormorants, fulmars, guillemots and gannets use the protection of steep cliffs to make their nesting sites.

Glossary

ABRASION The wearing away of a cliff by the scouring action of sand and pebbles carried in the surf.

ARCH A natural tunnel cut through a headland, usually by the growth of a cave. An example of an arch is Durdle Dor, Dorset (see its picture on page 1).

BACKWASH The flow of surf back down a beach.

BAR A ridge of sand that forms across an estuary, blocking off a river from the sea. Some wide bars are called barriers, and if a bar is split by channels into islands, each island is called a barrier island. An example of a bar is at Slapton Sands, Devon.

BARRIER ISLAND A long ridge of sand that has been driven ashore by waves and which forms long, thin islands offshore. They are uncommon in the UK, but very common in the eastern and southern United States, where they are sites for holiday resorts like Miami Beach, Florida.

BAY A natural, smoothly-curved inlet in the coast. Bays are formed in softer rocks and are bounded by headlands. Many bays have wide, sandy beaches.

BEACH A thin sheet of sand or pebbles that lies between the high and low-tide parts of a coast.

BREAKER A wave that reaches the coast and then rises steeply, so that the leading edge of the wave develops foam.

CAVE A natural hollow in a cliff, formed as a result of breaking waves crashing against the rocks. Most caves form where lines of weak rock are eroded by waves.

CLIFF A steep slope at the coast, often with a face of bare rock.

COAST The place where the land meets the sea.

COVE A very small bay, usually less than a kilometre or so across. Coves tend to occur within hard rock coasts. Cornwall is noted for its many "smugglers' coves".

DELTA The fan-shaped area of land that builds up where a river enters the sea and the sand and silt it is carrying settle out. The Mississippi delta is an example of a large delta.

DEPOSIT The settling out of material, such as sand, carried by waves or currents.

EROSION The wearing away and removal of land.

ESTUARY A drowned valley in a low lying coast. Estuaries were formed during the Ice Age when sea levels fell and rivers cut into their beds. At the end of the Ice Age the sea levels rose again and flooded the ends of the deepened valleys. The estuaries of the Thames, Wye, Severn and Humber are all examples of drowned valleys.

FJORD An inlet created by a glacier during the Ice Age and now flooded by the sea. The world's longest fjord is the Sogne fjord, which stretches 204km inland from the coast of Norway.

FLOTSAM Rubbish that people have dumped in the sea and which has floated onto the beach.

GROYNE A fence built out onto a beach to stop the natural drift of sand along the beach.

HEADLAND The parts of the coast that stand out into the sea. Most headlands are formed in hard rock.

ICE AGE The time when glaciers and ice sheets spread over the land. The water locked up in the ice caused the sea levels to fall, so that rivers and glaciers cut down into their former beds. When the Ice Age was over and sea levels rose once more, these valleys became flooded to make estuaries (river valleys) and fjords, sea lochs and sounds (glacial valleys).

LANDSLIDE A rapid movement of rock and soil down a cliff. This occurs more commonly in soft rocks, and especially after heavy rainfall.

LONGSHORE DRIFT The natural sawtooth movement of sand along a beach. It is caused by the different directions in which the swash and backwash moved. Longshore drift causes the formation of sand spits.

MUD The finest size of material carried by water. Mud will only settle out when conditions are calm, such as in an estuary. Mud builds up in estuaries to form mudflats.

MUDFLOW The rapid movement, as a flow of soil, rock and water, down a cliff.

OIL SLICK The trail of oil that is produced on the surface of the sea after an oil spill.

OIL SPILL The accidental or deliberate release of oil from a ship or storage tank. It is one of the most devastating forms of beach pollution.

POLLUTE To contaminate a healthy environment, such as a beach, and so threaten wildlife and people.

RIPPLE Small waves in sand that are seen on sandy beaches close to the low tide level.

SAND DUNE Mounds of sand that build up at the back of some wide beaches as a result of sand being blown inland off the beaches at low tide.

SAND SPIT A long, often curved, deposit of sand formed where the coast turns sharply, or where there is an estuary. Spits are formed because waves push material along the beach and do not change direction quickly. As a result, they continue to send material in the same direction as the beach, and this gradually builds up in the sea as a long beach. Large sand spits in the UK include Borth sands near Aberystwyth, Hurst Castle near Southampton and Spurn Head at the end of the river Humber, Lincolnshire.

SANDBANK A build-up of sand off the coast, often sufficient to produce a small island at low tide. Famous sandbanks include the Goodwin Sands off the coast of SE England.

SEA DEFENCE Any construction that people have built to try to slow down the natural erosion of the coast.

SEA LEVEL The average level of the sea.

SEA LOCH A drowned glacial valley in Scotland. Equivalent to fjord or sound. Loch Linnhie in western Scotland is an example of a large sea loch.

▼ **Waves crash against a stone sea wall built to protect houses from storms (Staithes, North Yorkshire).**

SEA WALL A vertical or very steep wall, usually of concrete, but sometimes of stone, that is built at the back of a beach to prevent storm waves from eroding the coast. It is usually built to protect houses in a seaside town.

SHINGLE A term used for pebbles on a beach.

SOUND A drowned glaciated valley. Equivalent to fjord, and this name is used in Canada and New Zealand. Milford Sound in South Island, New Zealand, is a large sound.

STACK A column of rock left standing seawards of a headland. The Old Man of Hoy, Orkney, is a dramatic example of a stack.

STEWARDSHIP The idea that we have a responsibility to keep the natural environment around us from being destroyed or damaged and so allow the planet to continue to

support future generations of people and wildlife.

SURF The region of foamy water where the waves break on a beach.

SUSTAINABLE DEVELOPMENT The kind of land use that will not cause irreparable harm, but which will be able to be adopted for the foreseeable future.

SWASH The landward movement of surf in a breaker.

TIDE The change in the level of the sea during the day.

TRANSPORT The movement of materials along a beach.

WAVE The part of the sea caught by the wind and driven inshore.

WAVE-CUT NOTCH A place where a cliff is cut away at the bottom as a result of wave action.

Index